101 Budget Britain Travel Tips

BY
Jonathan and Jacqueline Thomas
Anglotopia.net

CONTENTS

1 Planning   5

2 Transport   14

3 Lodging   36

4 Food   46

5 Attractions   56

6 Entertainment   74

7 Shopping   82

8 Communication   98

9 Other Tips   107

Appendix 1   117

Appendix 2   129

Welcome!
About This Book

It's no secret that Britain is an expensive place. We certainly know. After making nearly 10 trips to the UK over the last decade, we've seen the best and the worst that Britain has to offer in the budget travel realm.

We've experienced it all from luxury travel to running out of money while in country (on separate trips!).

We get questions every day from readers asking how they can make the best of their trip and do it on a budget. We also get comments from people who've written off a trip to Britain entirely because they think it's too expensive. That's a downright shame.

Britain may be expensive, but with careful planning and thought, you can travel there on a budget and still enjoy yourself. That's why we decided to write this guide - to help anyone planning or thinking of planning a trip to Britain save money so they can make it happen.

Happy Travels!

Jonathan & Jackie Thomas

Anglotopia.net

Chapter 1

PLANNING YOUR TRIP

Planning ahead is the best way to battle Britain's high tourist prices. The first section of this book will give you some tips on planning ahead to make the most of your trip to Britain from a budget travel perspective.

1. How To Set a Realistic Budget for Your Trip to Great Britain

The number one thing you can do to ensure that your trip goes smoothly is to plan ahead well in advance. Everything from where you are going to stay to what you are going to eat to what you are going to see – it all starts in the planning stages. When thinking about all of this, it is really important to start with the money you plan to spend and what will come out of these funds. For example, will your hotel bill come out of this or will that be paid ahead of time?

As you are planning the days of your trip, do some research. Many attractions and sites are free in England, such as most museums. Some attractions, such as the Tower of London, are not free. If you are staying in London in particular, keep in mind that it is one of the priciest cities in the world. That does not mean that it can't be done on a budget; you just really need to plan ahead. Once you know the cost of the attractions, set a loose itinerary and see how much it will cost you to see what you want to see.

Along with seeing the sights, you are going to have to plan how you will get to those sites. It is awesome if you are within walking distance, but what if you aren't? You can make your way around most cities cheaply using public transportation. Do some research here.

A lot of public transportation systems offer some sort of multiple ride program, and this may save you a lot of money. Another good thing to know is, when does public transport run? On one of my first trips abroad, I had a very early train to catch. I went to jump on the Tube in London only to see that it was closed! The Tube does not run 24 hours a day. I ended up having to take a cab, which was an unexpected expense.

One of the most important things in your budget is food. I have found myself thinking, "If I only eat one meal a day or just snack throughout the day, I will have more money to see things." In my experience, this is a huge mistake. You need to eat well. Set a realistic budget for food. A good hearty breakfast is a necessity, and also plan for a light lunch and a big dinner. There are many tips in the Budget Britain Guide on how to eat on the cheap. Do not deprive yourself food money for other things. You will end up hungry and feeling lousy. You want to be in top shape to see the sites, because there is usually a lot of walking involved. Make sure to stay hydrated, too!

Last but not least, make sure to leave a little "cushion" of funds for the unexpected. It really is a good idea to have some emergency funds should you need them for any reason. Make sure you can access these funds while you are abroad if necessary. They won't do you much good if you can't get to them.

Another word of caution here is be street smart when trying to cut costs. For instance, never take an unlicensed taxi cab in the hopes of getting a better deal. You won't!

Remember: Plan an itinerary deciding what you want to see; research entrance fees for attractions and the cost of transportation to get there; and set a good meal plan for yourself. With a little bit of planning and forethought, you can have a wonderful time on your vacation abroad.

Based on our experience, a good estimate for a trip to Britain centered on London is about $3,000- 4,000 USD. You can do it for cheaper, but that all depends on how much you want to suffer.

2. Beware of Bank Holiday Weekends

If you're going to be in Britain on a bank holiday weekend, be prepared for things to be closed, close early, and also be more expensive. A bank holiday is a public holiday in Britain where most of the country is off work – that is except people who work in tourist hotspots. It can also be more expensive to travel on these weekends as you'll have to share attractions, lodging, airplanes and the roads with other Brits – which means prices will be higher as they are peak travel times. While most museums and major attractions will be open, they usually keep special holiday hours (which will usually be the same as Sunday hours).

Here's a list of the usual bank holidays so you can avoid them:

- New Year's
- Good Friday
- Easter Monday
- May Bank Holiday (first week of May)
- Spring Bank Holiday (first week of June)
- Summer Bank Holiday (last Monday in August)
- Christmas Day
- Boxing Day

Some of the holidays will vary on their observance between Wales, Scotland and Northern Ireland. Check locally.

3. Watch out for Half-Term Deals

Britain's school kids usually get a one-week break in the middle of their semesters, and this time is called half-term. This means that Britain's popular tourist attractions will be mobbed with kids and families as they seek to take advantage of the days off.

While you'll have to contend with more crowds, keep a look out for special half-term deals. Many of the railways, museums, and other attractions will offer special half-term deals – even if you're from outside the country.

When is half-term time in Britain? That will depend on which part of Britain you're in, but here's a rough guide:

- Autumn term: Early September to mid December (half term: late October)

- Spring Term: Early January to Easter (half term: mid February)

- Summer Term: Easter to mid July (half term: late May/early June)

4. Protect Your Trip With Travel Insurance

Bad things happen. Flights get canceled. Hotels get overbooked. Natural disasters happen. While it's an added cost to your trip, you may want to consider getting some type of travel insurance.

Our biggest reason for recommending this is that if something happens and the onus isn't on your airline or hotel to fix the problem. If you're on a budget, how can you afford to get yourself out of a sticky situation?

You can expect to spend $100-200 per person for good travel insurance. It's worth the piece of mind.

5. Top 5 Free Things to do in Lincoln

Lincoln is most famous for its stunning cathedral, but there's plenty of other things to see and do in Lincoln that won't break the pocketbook. Here's our list of free things to do in Lincoln, England.

Lincoln Cathedral - You can enter free of charge and gaze at the nave, spend time of quiet in the Morning Chapel, or visit the shop. There is an admission charge for the rest of the cathedral.

The Collection - Visitors to historic Lincoln can enjoy a fabulous free-to-enter museum and the region's premier art gallery, the Usher.

Museum of Lincolnshire Life - Enjoy free entry to the largest and most diverse community museum in Lincolnshire.

Battle of Britain Memorial Flight Visitor Centre - While a little far out of town, you can explore Britain's rich aviation heritage here.

Explore Canals - Explore Lincoln's beautiful canals.

6. Top 5 Free Things to do in Norwich, England

Norwich is a lovely town near the North Sea that has many exciting attractions to visit. We've put together a list of our favorite free things to do in Norwich.

The Old Skating Rink Gallery - The South Asian Decorative Arts and Crafts Collection (SADACC) presents its extensive collection of the everyday arts, crafts and cultures of South Asia at the Old Skating Rink Gallery, only 50 metres from the Forum in Norwich.

Norwich Cathedral - Norwich's magnificent Romanesque Cathedral is open all day to visitors of all faiths and none. Set in beautiful grounds, it is an awe-inspiring and welcoming building. With spectacular architecture, magnificent art, and a fascinating history, it is well worth a visit.

The Forum - The Forum in Norwich is a stunning community building in the city centre and is the ideal place to meet any time of the year.

Sainsbury Centre for Visual Arts - The Sainsbury Centre for Visual Arts is an inspirational public art museum at the University of East Anglia (UEA), a short distance from Norwich city centre.

The Assembly House - In the heart of the city, this fine Georgian historic house is a leading venue for the arts, concerts, exhibitions, and meetings.

Chapter 2

TRANSPORT

This chapter will guide you through the ins and outs of traveling around Britain on it's various modes of transport. If you plan ahead and have the knowledge enclosed you can save a lot of money getting around Britain! Best of all - you can see far flung parts of Britain for an affordable price.

7. Book Your Flights on a Wednesday

When it comes to booking your airfare to Britain, there are a few things you can do to save some money. Here's our biggest suggestion: fly on a Wednesday.

Mid-week airfares are almost always lower than traveling on a weekend. You can also save money by flying on a Tuesday or a Thursday, but usually Wednesday is the cheapest day to fly to Britain.

British Airways has a great booking system that lets you see the airfare for each day of the week around your preferred date. This is an incredibly useful tool.

It can be inconvenient work-wise to book a vacation leaving mid-week, but you'll definitely save some money this way.

8. Travel With a Carry-On Bag Only

It's no secret that airlines are trying get every last penny they can get out of travelers, and one of their most innovative ways is to charge for your checked bags. Well, the joke's on them, because if you pack cannily, all you'll need is a carry-on bag for your trip. This is a great way to save money while flying to Britain. You'll also get through the airport much faster, as you won't have to wait for baggage reclaim.

The other passengers may hate you as your bag will take up more space in the overhead bin, but these days it's every traveler for himself!

The only problem with this plan is that most likely you will return with more than you left with in souvenirs and other purchases. Consider shipping those home or checking a souvenir-only bag.

9. Don't Fall for the Illusion of Free Travel with Airmiles

There's a big movement out there of people who claim to travel for free using airline rewards miles. I'm sure there are people who do this and can do quite well at it. But they are the exception, not the rule.

When it comes to traveling to Britain, our experience has been the airmiles are not worth the trouble.

Here's why: when you buy a plane ticket from any of the major airlines to Britain, your airfare is the smallest part of the ticket. For example, when we recently booked tickets to London from the USA, we spent $900 on each ticket with only $150 of that actually being our airfare – the rest was eaten up by taxes and fuel surcharges.

How does this affect flying for free with airmiles? Well, even if you have saved up enough miles to book a trip to Britain for free, you'll get sticker shock as only your actual airfare is free - you'll still have to pay all the taxes and fuel surcharges.

While you can save a little money this way, it's our opinion that the effort and expense required to take advantage of this is not really worth it. It can take years to earn enough airline miles. There's no way to travel for free these days, at least not to Britain.

10. The Cheapest Way to get to Central London from Heathrow

Well, walk. Just kidding.

The most affordable way to get into central London from Heathrow Airport is to simply take the London Underground. You can take the Piccadilly Line from Heathrow straight into central London for the cost of a cup of coffee. It will take about 40 minutes or so and can be inconvenient with luggage, but this is the cheapest way bar walking.

11. Get an Oyster Card

For the cheapest Tube fares in London, you must get an Oyster Card. An Oyster Card is a travel card that you load money on to travel the Tube and bus networks. Using the Oyster Card, you can save 50-60% on your Tube fare compared to paying cash. No matter how much you travel in a day, you'll always be charged the lowest possible fare, and paying with an Oyster Card is usually much cheaper than purchasing a day or week pass.

You can easily purchase them before you leave for London from Visit Britain Direct: http://www.visitbritaindirect.com/ or you can also buy one at many shops or Tube stations.

12. Where to Get a Free Tube Map

One of our favorite things to do is just look at the London Underground network map. We even used to have one on our wall as a poster. Having a copy of the map in your pocket is indispensable while in London as it's great to have a copy to look at whenever you need it.

So, where can you get a Tube Map for free?

Well, first you can get a free network map at pretty much any Tube station on the network. We recommend searching one out at the airport so you have it for your whole trip.

Second, you can get one in a tourist information office like the Visit Britain Tourist Information Centre at 1 Regent's Street in the west end.

Alternatively, you can print your own copy by downloading the latest version from Visit London:

http://www .visitlondon.com/maps/travel_maps/

13. Save Money With Budget Flights Within Britain

Easyjet and Ryanair offer cheap fares all around the British Isles, and it's a great way to fit in Edinburgh, Belfast or Dublin if you're on a budget. You can sometimes get a ticket for as little at £20.

But be warned, these airlines are the worst at charging extra fees that can end up making the journey cost more. If you're canny and avoid the fees, you can save a lot of money traveling this way.

Easyjet: http://www.easyjet.com/

Ryanair: http://www.ryanair.com/

14. A Guide to Ryanair's Fees

Ryanair is one of Europe's biggest discount airlines, and they can be a great way to get around Britain very cheaply – that is, if you book your ticket in a way to avoid their famous excessive fees. We've gathered their latest fees and have them below for your research, so you don't get sticker shock while you're traveling.

Admin Fee - Per passenger/per new one-way flight - relates to costs associated with Ryanair's booking system. £6

Priority Boarding Fee - Per passenger/per one-way flight. £5 Reserved Seating Fee - £10

Infant Fee - Per infant/per one-way flight (must be under 2 years for both outbound and return flight) £20

Infant Equipment - (car/booster/travel cot) Fee charged per item/per one-way flight. Maximum weight of 20kg per item. One pushchair per child carried free of charge. £10

Sports Equipment - Fee charged per item/per one-way flight. A maximum weight of 20kg per item.

(Bikes max weight – 30kg.) £50

Flight Change Fees - Per Passenger/per one-way flight. £50 Name Change Fee - Per Passenger. £110 Baggage fees vary based on weight and time of year. They start at £15 and go up to £50. These fees are current as of January 2012.

15. A Guide to EasyJet Fees

Like Ryanair, EasyJet is a great way to travel cheap by air around Britain. Also like Ryanair, EasyJet is notorious for ripping off consumers with their absurd fees. Here's a quick guide to them so you don't get taken for a ride.

All bookings will incur a £9.00 administration fee. Bookings made by Visa Credit Card, MasterCard, Diners Club, American Express, Carte Bleue (domestic transactions only) and UATP/Airplus will incur an additional fee of 2.5% of the total transaction value, with a minimum charge of £4.95, whichever is greater.

Paying for flight transfers and name changes to existing bookings by Carte Bleue, Visa Electron, ELV, Visa debit card, or Maestro/ Solo is free of charge. Payments made using Visa credit cards, MasterCard, American Express, Diners Club, or UATP/ AirPlus will incur a transaction fee of 2.5% of the total value of the flight and/or name changes.

Cancellation fee - £30 Name change fee - £35(online) Flight change fee - £35(online) Rescue fee - £50 Excess baggage fee - £10 per kilo over Sports equipment per flight - £25 (online)

Speedy Boarding - £14 Infant charge - £20 Admin fee - £9 Group booking fee - £4.50 per passenger Administration fee for insurance letters and printed flight confirmations - £10.

These fees are current as of January 2012.

16. Budget Trains: How to get £1 Train Tickets for All Over Britain

I wanted to share a little secret for those that enjoy traveling Britain by rails. If you want a very affordable way to get around the country, check out Megatrain.com. Train tickets start at £1 (plus a .50p booking fee).

You can travel all over via Southwest Trains and the East Midlands line. Prices are low, because they're looking to fill seats on empty trains. If you book in advance, you can lock a deal.

The only catch is that you can only go to very specific destinations, and the fare rules are much different than regular trains. For example, some trains have designated train cars with restricted exits. However, by playing by the rules, savings can be substantial.

Megatrain offers low-cost intercity train travel on East Midlands Trains and Southwest Trains, both of which are owned by Stagecoach Group. In addition, Megabusplus tickets allow combined coach and train journeys to London via East Midlands Parkway railway station with Feeder services from Huddersfield - Halifax - Bradford, Harrogate - York - Castleford and Hull – Scunthorpe.

17. Save Money on Rail Fares - The Britrail Pass

The Britrail Pass is something that's only available to those who live outside of Britain. It's a pass that basically gives you unlimited travel on Britain's rail network for a set period of time.

They can be expensive, but if you plan to do extensive travel of Britain's rail networks, they can pay for themselves very quickly.

You have to buy your pass before you arrive in Britain as you cannot buy them there (wouldn't want the Brits to get these great deals, do we?)

More info: http://www.britrail.com/

18. First Class Means FIRST CLASS in Britain

One of the weird things to get used to in Britain is that their classes of travel are very rigid. Many trains - even commuter trains - have first class cabins, which is rather strange in itself.

Unless you have a first class ticket, you cannot go into the first class cabin. Even if it's empty. If you're caught, you could be forced to pay an on-the-spot fine or have to buy a first class ticket. Rest assured, your ticket will be checked by the conductor.

First class tickets on short journeys don't usually cost that much more than regular tickets, so if you want a little more legroom and a quieter ride, consider traveling first class. Just don't consider trying to do it for free.

19. Skip the Train and Ride the Bus Instead

If you want to get around Britain cheaply, there's another option that doesn't get as much attention as Britain's trains: the bus (or the coach, as they say in Britain).

Britain has a vast intercity bus network, and you can get around Britain very cheaply this way. For example, you can get from London to Edinburgh for under £50 if you book far enough in advance (try finding train fares that cheap - you won't!).

You may groan at the idea of spending a couple of days on a bus, but you probably won't. Remember, Britain is a small country, and you can drive between most major cities within a day or less. The bus trip from London to Edinburgh is just 9 hours, for example.

If you can handle the swaying of the buses and want to see Britain's motorways instead of its railways, give the bus a try.

We recommend looking at Megabus first: http://uk.megabus.com/

20. Always Use a Licensed Taxi - Not Just in London

Wherever you are in Britain and need to use a taxi service, always use a licensed taxi service. Never use a mini-cab or other unlicensed service.

It's a safety issue and a cost issue.

Licensed taxi services have to give you the best fare to your destination, and they're heavily regulated because of this. They also have to be trained in their local area on where everything is (in London they call this "the knowledge").

Mini-cabs and other unlicensed cabs aren't held to the same standards, and they can charge whatever fares they want. It's also very unsafe to ride in an unlicensed taxi.

If you need to take a taxi, always be on the lookout for a licensed cab. In major cities this will be obvious. In smaller towns, you might have to ask, but your safety and pocketbook are worth it.

21. Don't Rent a GPS from the Car Rental Company

If you plan to rent a car while in Britain, we don't recommend renting a GPS navigation unit (the Brits call them Sat-navs) from the car rental company. They can cost $20-30 a day to rent, which is really expensive for something so simple.

It's tempting, though. A device that will direct you exactly where you need to go on Britain's confusing spaghetti roads? But as long as you have a good roadmap or an iPhone (GPS is free, maps will cost you data roaming so plot your trip out on WiFi before setting off), you don't need to spend the money on an already expensive car rental for the privilege of driving directions.

I always have the spouse navigate with the roadmap. It's more fun this way anyway!

22. Watch out for Car Rental Insurance Rip-offs

If you rent a car in Britain, it's understandable to want to get as much car insurance as possible so you're protected. But this is a quick way to waste a lot of money.

Your fee for renting the car actually includes basic insurance. Anything they sell you is extra and probably unneeded in most cases.

Your rental quote will normally include basic coverage, including third-party coverage, vehicle damage coverage, collision damage insurance, and vehicle theft coverage. This is all that's required by law in the UK. The rest is a risk you can take. Your credit card may also cover beyond the minimums.

We fell for the car rental insurance scam when we rented a car for the first time, and it almost doubled the cost of our car rental. We're not doing that again.

23. Watch out for the Congestion Charge in London

Several years ago, London instituted a congestion charge in central London for all cars that enter the congestion charge zone. If a car enters the congestion charge zone, it has to pay a toll of £10 during the week during daylight hours (weekends and holidays there is no charge).

It's supposed to reduce traffic in Central London. As tourists, we haven't really noticed much of a difference in traffic, and it really seems like more of a cash grab for the London government.

That said, even if you're renting a car, you are still responsible for paying the charge. If you don't, you could end up with the charge on your car rental bill with some added penalties from the car rental company (especially if you don't do it on time).

So, if you drive your rental into London, go online and pay your charge right away. We've heard horror stories of travelers who got huge bills from their rental company for forgetting (or just not knowing).

Congestion Charge:

http://www.tfl.gov.uk/roadusers/congestioncharging/

24. Cheap Way to Get Around London - Bike Rental from the Barclays Cycle Hire Scheme

If you want a really cheap way to get around London, consider renting a bike from the Barclays Cycle Hire Scheme. The bikes are located all around London, and anyone can register to rent a bike. You ride it to the next station and return it. It's a great way to see London on a bike – if you're brave enough to face London's clogged and dangerous streets.

Another bonus: it's cheaper than a taxi!

You can sign up online to access the system, or you can pay for your rental on the spot at the bike terminals. It costs £1 to access the system, then you're charged £1 for the first hour. The first 30 minutes are free, so all you pay is the access fee if your trip takes under 30 minutes. It's a great deal. You can get to a lot of places in central London in 30 minutes.

Check the website for more details:

http://www.tfl.gov.uk/roadusers/cycling/14808.aspx

25. Cross the Thames for Free in the Greenwich Foot Tunnels

If you want a fun experience and don't want to pay to cross the Thames into Greenwich on the Tube, consider using the free Victorian-era foot tunnels that cross under the river.

The Greenwich Foot Tunnel is a pedestrian tunnel under the Thames that runs between Greenwich and Island Gardens on the other side of the river. There are about a hundred steps at each end, but it's free and open 24 hours a day. The tunnel just went through a refurbishment, and there are new elevators if you don't want to brave the stairs.

The Woolwich foot tunnel is a tunnel crossing under the River Thames in East London from Woolwich in the London Borough of Greenwich to North Woolwich in the London Borough of Newham. There are currently no lifts while the tunnel is being renovated. There's also free ferry you can take as well called the Woolwich Free Ferry.

We've done this one, and it was a lot of fun!

26. Just Walk to Save Some Money

This tip is for London in particular: consider walking to your destination instead of taking public transportation. London is a big city and has plenty of options for inexpensive transportation, but sometimes it is just nicer to walk. I am speaking particularly of the Tube. While it is fast and inexpensive, it is almost entirely underground in London. You miss so many of the sights traveling completely underground.

The Tube maps show the location of stations slightly skewed. Some are actually quite close together, and you can easily walk between them. However, stations with many connections, like Bank, are so large that you might not want to walk. Either way, walking the streets of London allows you to really see the city. Who knows what gems you might uncover on a stroll.

If you get a bit lost, don't panic. Have a good pocket map with you, and you can always politely ask a passerby for directions to where you are going. Make some time to walk above ground while you are in London, because there is a lot to miss if you stay underground the entire time.

27. Top 5 Free Things to do in Glasgow, Scotland

Glasgow is Scotland's second city, and it's recently gone through a bit of a renaissance. There's much to see and do culturally, and we've put together a list of the top 5 free things to do in Glasgow, Scotland.

Riverside Museum of Transport - The dynamic new Riverside Museum displays Glasgow's rich industrial heritage, which stems from the River Clyde.

St Mungo Museum of Religious Art - The award-winning St Mungo Museum is a haven of tranquillity in a bustling city. Its galleries are full of displays, artifacts and stunning works of art.

Kelvingrove Art Gallery and Museum - Kelvingrove Art Gallery and Museum is one of Scotland's most popular free attractions. Kelvingrove has 22 themed, state-of-the-art galleries displaying an astonishing 8,000 objects.

Gallery of Modern Art - As the centre for Glasgow's modern art collection, its changing displays are inspired by what the City owns.

Glasgow Cathedral - The first stone-built Glasgow Cathedral was dedicated in the presence of King David I in 1136. The present building was consecrated in 1197. Since that same period, the Cathedral has never been unroofed and the worship of God has been carried out within its walls for more than 800 years.

28. Top 5 Free Things to do in Cardiff

Cardiff is one of Britain's most vibrant capital cities and recently invested millions in turning around its seafront. There's much to see and do these days, and we've put together a list of the top 5 free things you can do in Cardiff Wales.

The National Museum & Gallery, Cardiff - History, science and the arts at your fingertips, the National Museum & Gallery really captures your imagination. It houses the best collection of impressionist paintings outside of Paris.

The National Assembly for Wales Visitors Centre - You can learn more about Wales and Cardiff itself at the National Assembly For Wales Visitors Centre at the Pierhead and Cardiff Bay Visitors Centre.

St Fagans National History Museum - St Fagans National History Museum, is one of Europe's foremost open-air museums representing the life and culture of Wales. Situated in 100 acres of parkland, the museum also has displays of costume, daily life and farming implements.

Bay Art Gallery - The Bay Art Gallery on Bute Street promotes major exhibitions by Welsh and International Artists.

Cardiff Summer Festival - The city is also host to one of the UK's largest free festivals, the Cardiff Summer Festival.

Chapter 3

LODGING

After your airfare to Britain, your hotel or lodging will be your next most expensive cost. Armed with these tips, you can make sure it doesn't hit the pocket book too hard.

29. The Lowdown on Budget Hotels in Britain

One of the biggest costs of any trip is lodging. Hotel prices in the UK can be outrageous! You can find a great deal on a nice hotel, but there are some pitfalls to avoid. Here are a few tips on budget lodging in the UK.

Check the Neighborhood - Yes, you may have found a super nice hotel for a great price, but if the price seems too good to be true, it probably is! This is pretty common. The neighborhood may not be necessarily a "bad" area – it may be too far out, too. You will not save any money staying outside of the city center, because you are going to spend more in the long run commuting back and forth. Speaking from experience, commuting back and forth from the hotel is a real bummer.

Read Reviews - We always read reviews before we stay anywhere, no matter the price point. You have to read reviews with a critical eye. Some people are really finicky about certain things and can give a hotel a bad score unnecessarily. There are only two things that will put us off in reviews – bed bugs and dirty rooms. However, we have to see this type of complaint more than once in many reviews before we take it to heart.

When to Check Out - If you get to your hotel, and it is downright scary, don't immediately panic. You got a good deal on the room for a reason. The questions to ask yourself are: Will I be safe here? Is the room too dirty? Are there bedbugs?

Rude Staff - A British friend and I were talking a while back, and we joked that in the United States the customer is always right, and in the UK the customer is always wrong. Rude staff isn't always the case, but we have pretty much come to expect it. This is not a reason to leave your hotel. Just try to be polite and go your own way.

Not all budget lodging is scary. Honestly, we have only had one less than desirable experience while staying in the UK; the room was dirty and the hotel was noisy. We stayed there for the duration of the trip, because we didn't spend a lot of time in my room. That is the moral of the story here: you didn't travel abroad to spend all of your time in your room. Get out and see what you came to see. You simply need somewhere to sleep and wash in a safe environment. Read reviews and do your homework before you stay, and you will do okay.

30. What are the Cheapest, Cleanest Hotels in London?

The cheapest and cleanest hotels in London are the EasyHotel chain of hotels located in South Kensington, Paddington, Victoria, Heathrow, Earl's Court, Luton and the City.

Rooms are very basic, offering just a bed and a bathroom. There are no amenities, and you even have to pay for the privilege of watching the TV. However, rooms are clean, comfortable and in safe neighborhoods.

Rates start at £25 a night if you book far enough in advance, which is a great deal for London!

31. Consider a B&B Over a Hotel

If you're looking to save money on lodging in the UK, you might want to consider staying in a bed and breakfast. You get to stay with locals, get that personal connection, and breakfast is included. In rural areas of Britain that aren't well served by hotels, B&Bs are a great alternative.

We've stayed in a few B&Bs. We have always enjoyed ourselves, and the pocket was hit a little less hard than if we stayed in a hotel. You won't save much if you stay in B&Bs in London, but elsewhere in Britain and in the countryside, you can save a lot.

32. Consider Staying in a Hostel to Save Money in Britain

This option is more popular with students and younger people than more seasoned travelers, but you can save a lot of money by staying in a youth hostel instead of a hotel.

Staying in a hostel requires a little bit of sacrifice as you sometimes have to share a room – as well as a bathroom. The trade-off is that you get a cheap place to sleep, and you meet a lot of interesting people from around the world. You can find a bed as low as $10-20 a night.

If you do opt for a hostel, keep your wits about you and guard your valuables. There are people who prey on hostelers (seeing them as easy marks). As long as you watch out, you should be safe.

Good place to look for hostels:
http://www.hostelbookers.com/

33. Stay in Someone's Apartment or House and Live Like a Local with AirBNB

Staying in a flat while traveling isn't a new travel trend, but AirBNB has totally changed things. Instead of only companies offering flats for let, people are now letting out rooms in their apartments or houses. You can also rent an entire property.

Prices can be pretty cheap depending on where you're willing to stay and what kind of accommodations you need. Availability will be strange and change every time you do a search, so if you see something you want, book it right away. They've got listings all over the UK, so you'll easily find something no matter where you want to travel in Britain.

AirBNB also has lots of safeguards built in so you don't end up with nowhere to stay if something goes wrong. If you want to make some money while you're in Britain, you can even rent out your own home while you're gone.

Check it out: http://airbnb.com

34. The Glories of Couchsurfing - Staying for Free in Britain

If you're really on a budget and basically want somewhere to stay for free while you're in Britain, consider joining the website Couchsurfing.org.

Couchsurfing is a travel social network where people offer their couches or spare beds to weary travelers for free. It's a way to grow your network of friends and gain a new experience.

We've heard a lot of good things about this method of travel, but it's not something we've ever done. With something like this, safety is paramount, so do be careful.

Website: http://www.couchsurfing.org/

35. Top 5 Free Things to do in Manchester, England

There are many attractions worth seeing in Manchester if you're on a budget. Here are our five favorite free attractions in England's industrial heartland of Manchester.

Manchester Town Hall - A symbol of Victorian Age architecture, this building is a marvel to behold.

Manchester Cathedral - Unlike others in the UK, you don't have to pay to get in and have a look around.

Museum of Science and Industry - Great museum dedicated to to the industrial revolution with many exciting displays.

Manchester Art Gallery - Great collection of British and European art that just reopened after a major renovation.

Castlefield Urban Heritage Park - Great collection of buildings from a rebuilt Roman Fort, world's oldest train station, first industrial canal and much more!

36. Top 5 Free Things to do in Liverpool, England

Liverpool is one of Britain's biggest cities, and there is much to do for the tourist. Here are five attractions in Liverpool that are free.

Liverpool Cathedral - Another one of Britain's beautiful cathedrals that's free to enter and have a wander around.

Albert Dock - Great area of regeneration with lots to see and do that doesn't cost a dime.

Tate Liverpool - A lovely museum of contemporary and modern art in a fantastic setting.

Merseyside Maritime Museum - Explore Liverpool's rich maritime history in this dedicated museum.

International Slavery Museum - While the topic is not the most uplifting, explore the history of the modern age through slavery.

Chapter 4

FOOD

Britain has a huge variety of food, and if you're not careful, you'll spend a lot of money on your trip just eating to sustain yourself. Using these tips, you can offset that cost while still enjoying the best food Britain has to offer.

37. Find a Local Grocery Store or Snack Shop

If you are traveling on a budget, this tip is an absolute must. When you arrive or shortly thereafter, find a grocery store or corner shop that sells packaged food. Look for snacks like fruit, prepackaged crackers, or cookies. We highly recommend trying the "crisps," also known as chips. They come in some really interesting and amazingly delicious flavors.

You may even want to visit your local grocery store before you leave and bring some food from home for snacks. Just make sure that whatever you bring is prepackaged and still sealed, or you will have trouble getting it through customs. We brought a box of cereal once and just ran to the local store for single pints of milk for breakfast. We ate cereal out of the teacups that were provided in our room, and we were even able to pick up a bunch of bananas to go with our cereal for a healthy and inexpensive breakfast.

If you are bringing food from home, just remember to avoid liquids. Food must be sealed in its original packaging, and you cannot bring any fresh fruit or vegetables. If you are shopping while you are in the UK, remember you will most likely not have means of refrigeration or a way to cook most food items. Check your hotel room first to see what you have available to you for cooking and storage purposes, then venture out to the store.

38. Breakfast on the Cheap in London and Britain

Eating out for breakfast in Britain can be very expensive. While there's nothing better than a good English fry-up, our top tip for getting breakfast on the cheap is to stock up on breakfast foods when you arrive.

When we hit a local grocery store, we always buy breakfast provisions for the trip, including bananas, muffins, bottled water and any other food snacks that don't need to be cooked or refrigerated.

It's great. We have everything we need for a quick breakfast in the room so we can hit the ground running in the morning and be good until lunch. We usually spend £10-20 doing this, and we're good on breakfast for the whole trip!

39. Free Tea!

Most hotels rooms will provide you with a tea kettle and tea. Take advantage of this before leaving your room rather than paying for a cuppa while you're out and about. Tea will be the lifeblood of your trip.

40. Why Not Share a Meal?

A great way to save money for an expensive dinner out is to share a meal. Most food portions in Britain are bigger than one person can eat, so simply ask for an extra plate and split your plate with your travel partner.

Some restaurants may not allow this, so be sure to ask first.

To take best advantage of this, order a starter, main course and dessert and share them all. You'll have to eat the same thing as your partner, but you've saved the cost of two meals.

41. A Dirt Cheap Lunch - Ready Made Sandwiches

Britain invented the sandwich, and that's very clear in Britain today. Most convenience stores and food stores in places like railway stations stock a huge array of cheap, ready-made sandwiches. This is a great way to save money on lunch, and you can find them almost anywhere.

When we travel by train, we like to grab a sandwich in the station, and then have an impromptu picnic. It's a hearty lunch, and you won't pay a fortune for it.

The big chain stores will have the cheapest sandwiches, but you can get higher quality sandwiches at places like Au Bon Pain or EAT. Be sure to try some uniquely British sandwich combinations.

42. To Save Money - Just Don't Tip At All in Britain

If you're traveling on a budget and concerned about your money while in Britain, consider just not tipping. Tipping isn't as commonplace in Britain as it is in the USA, and it's very difficult to judge when it's appropriate. No one will think any worse of you if you don't tip at all.

Most restaurants put a service charge in the bill already. For other services, if you're never going to see the person again, what does it matter if you don't tip them? However, if you will be utilizing a person's services again in the course of your trip, and they did a good job, it's not a bad idea to tip anyway. But for most situations, hold onto your pence.

43. Fast Food is Your Friend - No Shame in McDonald's

While it's not the healthiest way to eat while you're traveling, eating fast food while in Britain will save you a lot of money. You can usually eat a tasty and filling meal for under £5.

You benefit from not going into a restaurant with waiter service. You'll pay a premium for waiter service, and most likely experience bad service anyway.

Whether it's going to McDonald's (which tastes better in Britain) or hitting up the local fish and chips shop, fast food is by far the most affordable way to eat in Britain.

One strange note, though: McDonald's in Britain does not really have breakfast (especially hotcakes).

44. Don't Wait to Eat at the Airport

This is more of a general budget traveling tip rather than one specifically for Britain, but it's simple: don't eat at airports.

Airports have captive customers, so prices don't have to be low. You'll even overpay at somewhere like McDonald's. To avoid high prices, either eat a good meal before you go to the airport or pack a lunch and eat it before you go through security.

We made the mistake of waiting to eat at the airport, and we were disappointed at how terrible the food was and shocked at how much we spent for the privilege to eat it.

45. Top 5 Free Things to do in Bristol, England

Bristol is a lovely seaside town on England's west coast, and there's much to see and do. Here's a list of five free things you can do that we discovered!

M Shed - A former warehouse in Bristol's docks has been turned into a museum dedicated to its rich maritime history.

Bristol Museum & Art Gallery - Bristol Museum & Art Gallery tells the story of our world in every display – from the beginning of time to the present day.

Clifton Suspension Bridge - The world famous Clifton Suspension Bridge was designed by the great Victorian engineer Isambard Kingdom Brunel.

Bristol Blue Glass Factory & Shop - Bristol Blue Glass Factory & Shop shows off the famous glassworks that have been synonymous with the city of Bristol for the past four centuries.

Bristol Cathedral - A magnificent gothic cathedral that dates back to the 1100s with free admission.

46. Top 5 Free Things to do in Nottingham, England

Nottingham is steeped in history, and that means there is plenty to do on a budget. Here's our list of free things you can do in Nottingham, England.

Green's Windmill and Science Centre - Green's Windmill in Sneinton was built by the father of notable scientist and mathematician George Green in 1807. Today the working Mill is a popular museum and science centre, which teaches new generations of children about the valuable work of George Green.

Wollaton Hall & Deer Park - Wollaton Hall is a spectacular Elizabethan mansion in the heart of Nottingham. It is a prominent Grade One listed building, and visitors of all ages are welcome to visit the hall and park.

Angel Row Gallery - This is a lively contemporary art gallery with a program of exhibitions that covers painting, photography, video and installations.

Galleries of Justice Museum - Based at Nottingham's old courthouse and gaol, there are many ways to explore the Galleries of Justice museum.

Nottingham Contemporary - Nottingham Contemporary, designed by the award-winning architects Caruso St John, is one of the largest contemporary art centres in the UK. It has four galleries lit by 132 skylights, a performance and film space, a learning room, the Study, the shop and Cafe.Bar.Contemporary.

Chapter 5

ATTRACTIONS

This is why you've come to Britain! Many of the major tourist attractions are pretty expensive, but using these tips you can save some money and make sure you still get to enjoy the best Britain has to offer without paying full price.

47. Top 5 Tourist Attractions to Avoid in London

Here's our list of overrated London attractions worth skipping due to cost and the crowds:

- London Dungeon (tourist trap)

- Madame Tussaud's (tourist trap)

- Westminster Abbey — St Paul's is more impressive.

- Buckingham Palace – It's a house, closed most of the year, and the changing of the guard is a tourist mob.

- British Library – It's just a library in a slightly dodgy neighborhood.

48. Just What are 'Concessions' Anyway?

In America, we're used to getting discounts for being part of some kind of group – be it a student discount or a senior discount. In the UK they call them concessions.

When you see pricing for concessions, that means there is a special kind of discount with it - if you meet the requirements, you can get it.

Be prepared to prove it, though!

49. Budget Tip: Don't Forget Your Student ID

If you're still pretty young and held onto your Student ID from your college or high school days, then take it with you. Many paid tourist attractions offer student discounts.

The discount sometimes isn't much, but every penny helps in an expensive place like Britain. Most of the time you won't even have to show your ID, but if you do, it's nice to have it. Some attractions might require an International Student Card, but your school ID should suffice at most locations.

Keep in mind, though: some things, like train tickets, have an age limit on student fares, so this trick won't work there.

50. Free British Travel Resources: Tourist Information Centres

Britain has a huge network of Tourist Information Centres usually located in areas of interest to tourists. They're a great local resource staffed by locals who know the most about their area.

You can usually pick up free local tourist materials, brochures, maps, etc. You can also ask the helpful people questions about travel in the area, and they'll be happy to help you out.

They're also able to help book local accommodation and give you advice on what to avoid. Most of them don't have websites, so just look out for their trademark signage or ask around in town. If you can find the phone number in advance, you can also call and get information over the phone to help you plan your trip in advance.

You can find a huge list of TICs here:
http://www.britainexpress.com/TIC/

51. How to See Britain's Cathedrals For Free - Attend Evensong Services

If you want to see the inside of Britain's famous cathedrals for free, all you need to do is wait until the tourist hours are over and attend an actual church service.

Choral evensong is free, and you get to see the cathedral for free. After they close the cathedrals to tourists, you can still come in and see the nightly service, usually held around 5pm. You can probably even have a wander once services are over.

You get to hear beautiful music and then see cathedral for free. Can't beat that, even if you're not religious. If you're in London, we recommend Westminster Abbey and St Paul's Cathedral. Outside of London, we recommend Salisbury Cathedral, Durham Cathedral and Yorkminster. Check with each cathedral as evening service times will vary.

52. Free Fun: London's Parks

We have traveled to London almost a dozen times and have seen pretty much every attraction, paid and free. However, despite all of the amazing things we've seen, Hyde Park in London has to be practically our favorite place on the face of this Earth. London is full of free parks, squares and gardens that are just as beautiful.

London's parks make a great place to visit. You can rest under a shady tree, take an awesome picnic, or just sit and people watch. Parks are also wonderful places to visit if you have children; it's a nice place to let them run off some energy.

Do a little research, and get yourself a good map of London. Most of the parks are open year round, and they always have something new to see. Some attractions, like the Winter Wonder Fest in Hyde Park, aren't free, but there is so much more to see of the park that is free. Take some time, take a stroll, and really enjoy London's parks, squares and gardens.

53. Budget Tip: Join the National Trust for Free Entry to Thousands of Properties

If you intend to visit a lot of Britain's historic homes and castles, it may be wise to consider a membership in the National Trust, which can get you free access to all their properties.

The National Trust is an organization in Britain that preserves Britain's heritage, and they own thousands of properties. If you're not a member, you have to pay for access to charging properties (like Churchill's House - Chartwell). These admissions can add up to quite a bit!

With a membership to the National Trust, access to all these properties is included. If you're an American, you need to join the Royal Oak Society, which is their sister organization in the USA. It costs just $55 per year for a membership, and it will pay for itself in one day of visits.

http://www.royal-oak.org/

http://www .nationaltrust.org.uk/

54. Budget Tips: Consider Getting an English Heritage Overseas Visitor Pass

Like the National Trust, English Heritage runs hundreds of historic properties throughout the UK, some which have pretty steep admission prices. Luckily for the overseas traveler, they offer an Overseas Visitor Pass that offers discounted entry into all their properties.

The Overseas Visitor Pass from English Heritage includes free entry to over 100 stately homes, castles, abbeys, Roman and prehistoric remains. With a pass, you can visit all attractions directly managed by English Heritage free of charge. It also includes free or reduced price entry to hundreds of action-packed events, as well as a 290-page color souvenir guidebook containing maps, information on over 100 staffed attractions, and a further 300 free attractions in the care of English Heritage.

Prices start at £21.50 for a 7-day pass and £26.00 for a 14-day pass (this is obviously the better deal). There are further options for families and children.

More info here:

http://www.english-heritage.org.uk/daysout/overseas-visitor-pass/

55. For Entry to Welsh Castles - Consider the Cadw Explorer Pass

If you plan to spend a lot of time in Wales, it's not a bad idea to get their equivalent to the National Trust or English Heritage Pass - the Cadw Explorer Pass.

Cadw's 3- or 7-day Explorer passes provide a great value way to explore the wealth of historic attractions Wales has to offer. The passes offer groups the freedom to explore as many of Cadw's historic attractions as they wish or can squeeze in during a visit to Wales. The 3-day pass can be used in any 7-day period, and the 7-day pass in any 14 days.

Retail Prices

3-day pass:

- Single Adult - £13.20

- Two Adults - £20.30

- Family - £28

7-day pass:

- Single Adult - £19.85

- Two Adults - £31.60

- Family - £38.75

56. Take a Cheap Cruise on the Thames with the Tate-to-Tate

If you're looking for a great way to see London but don't want to pay for the high-priced boat tours, consider taking the Tate-to-Tate boat ride. It's an all day boat service that runs from the Tate Modern to the Tate Britain. The Tate Boat runs every 40 minutes during gallery opening hours between Tate Britain and Tate Modern. You'll get to see a huge chunk of London from the Thames, and you get the added bonus of going to a great museum at the end.

It only costs £5.50 for one day (about $8 USD or so). It's even cheaper if you have an Oyster Card (which you should have!).

See website for current rates and timetables: http://www.tate.org.uk/tatetotate/

57. Train Travel: Get 2-for-1 Entry to Britain's Attractions if You Travel By Train

Britain's Rail Operators have a great ongoing deal for people who use the trains to get to Britain's top tourist attractions. They offer 2-for-1 entry if you use a train ticket.

They've got lots of fantastic 2FOR1 attraction offers and some great deals on train travel, including GroupSave where 3 or 4 people can travel together Off-Peak for the price of 2 adults to hundreds of destinations!

Your first step to get the offer is to browse the website and find the relevant attraction and related coupon. All you have to do is sign up on their website, fill in the details of your journey, and you'll get a voucher for use to get into the attraction. Easy as pie!

Days Out Guide Website:

http://www.daysoutguide.co.uk/

58. The Cheapest Bus Tour in London - The Heritage Line

Most of the classic London Double Decker Routemasters have been taken out of service, but they still run them on two bus lines in Central London. This is a great way to get a bird's-eye tour of London for the cost of a single bus ticket – about £2.

The classic Routemasters run on the bus routes 9 and 15. It's really affordable and fun to hop on, climb to the top, and ride the bus as it circles through all the London sights. It's also much less expensive than other bus "tours." You can get the same treatment on any London double-decker bus, but the Routemasters have a lot of history.

Carry a guidebook with you so you can read up on the landmarks you pass or just sit back and enjoy the sights and sounds of London as they pass by below you.

59. Free British Audio Tours - Rick Steves' Audio Europe App

Rick Steves has released a great free app for travelers that's perfect for a trip to Britain. It features a ton of audio content that you can use for free.

The app includes segments from Rick Steves' radio show as well as some of his classic walking tours. They make a great companion to his guidebooks.

Just for London alone there's 9 walking tours in the app and they're all FREE! There's also a great variety of audio for things to do beyond London.

I'm not sure why they're giving the app away as it's filled with tons of valuable content. The tours feature images to guide you around - really helpful.

You can download the app for iPhone or for Android, so there's wide platform availability. Rick also provides free maps you can download and print of the walking tour route.

Download it here:

http://www.ricksteves.com/ae/ae_menu.htm

60. Consider the London Pass for Savings in London

The London Pass is a great way to save money on your next trip to London. London is known as one of the most expensive cities in the world to visit, and its popular tourist attractions are no exceptions. If you're traveling in a family, entrance fees to various attractions can add up quickly and give you quite a surprise that you didn't budget for. That's where the London Pass comes in.

The London Pass gives you free access to most of London's top tourist attractions so that your attraction costs are fixed before you go to London. Conveniently, you can also get transport on the London Underground bundled into the card so you can save on getting around. Some of the attractions London Pass works with are actually already free – but you get added benefits such as free audio tours or guidebooks. With every purchase of a London Pass, you'll be given a great little guidebook that lists all the attractions and how to get to them. It's a great buy that we always recommend. Buy it with transport included for added savings.

Don't bother with a 1-day pass. It's not worth it as you won't have time to go to more than a couple attractions in a day. Buy at least a 3-day pass. 6-day passes are the best deal all around and give you plenty of time. Some attractions they advertise are already free to get in, but having a pass gets you a benefit like an audio tour or free guidebook when you get there. Buy several weeks before your planned trip.

61. Cheap London Guided Walks

If you're not careful, you'll end up paying an arm and a leg for a guided walking tour in London. Many people book guided tours through their airline or their hotel. Do not do this if you're on a budget, as you'll overpay.

We recommend London Walks instead – a company in London that's been around for a long time and offers a ton of different London walks at very affordable rates.

Their daily walks cost just £8, and you don't need to reserve a spot – just show up. Walks take about two hours. £8 is not bad for two hours of entertainment. They also offer day trips outside of London that cost £14 (plus train fare).

Here's a sampling of their London Walks:

Jack the Ripper Tour Day Trips from London The Olympics Walks Ghost Walks Harry Potter Walk The Royal Wedding Walk And more!

Check their website for tours and times:

http://www.walks.com/

62. Top 5 Free Things to do in Birmingham, England

Birmingham England has a rich industrial heritage, and there's much to see and do in one of England's biggest cities outside of London. Here's our picks of the best free things to see and do in Birmingham, England.

Victoria Square, Birmingham - One of the great public squares in Britain. Enjoy the fountains, people watching and beautiful architecture.

Birmingham Museum and Art Gallery - One of Britain's finest history and art museums. It has a collection of international importance covering fine art, ceramics, metalwork, jewelry, archaeology, ethnography, local history and industrial history.

Weoley Castle - The ruins at Weoley Castle are over 700 years old and are the remains of the moated medieval manor house that once stood here.

Ikon Gallery - A world-class modern art gallery in the center of Birmingham.

Birmingham Cathedral - The city's beautiful baroque cathedral.

63. Top 5 Free Things to do in Newcastle, England

Newcastle is a fine northern city in Britain, and there's plenty to see and do. We thought we'd put together a list of the top free things to see in do if you're on a budget and happen to be in Newcastle.

BALTIC Centre for Contemporary Art - Housed in a landmark industrial building on the south bank of the River Tyne in Gateshead, BALTIC is the biggest gallery of its kind in the world presenting a dynamic, diverse and international program of contemporary visual art.

The Angel of the North - The Gateshead Angel of the North is Britain's largest sculpture, designed by Antony Gormley for Gateshead Council. It weighs 200 tons, is 20m high and has a 54m wing span. T

Great North Museum: Hancock - Highlights of the new museum include a large-scale, interactive model of Hadrian's Wall.

Church of St Nicolas - Stunning Cathedral in a magical setting.

Discovery Museum - At Discovery Museum find out about life in Newcastle and Tyneside from the area's renowned maritime history and world-changing science and technology right through to fashion through the eras and military history.

Chapter 6

ENTERTAINMENT

These tips will guide you in finding the best deals to on entertainment while you're traveling in Britain.

64. Where to Get Half Price Theatre Tickets in London

Check out the Tkts Half-Price Ticket Booth located in Leicester Square (which is in the heart of Theatreland). This is the place to check for cheap theatre ticket deals before you check anywhere else as they are "official."

There will be many other places that purport to sell half-price tickets, but the one in Leicester Square is run by the actual theaters, and it's where they unload unsold seat inventory, so check there first.

You can also check out the official website at http://www.tkts.co.uk/ for the latest deals.

65. Best Places in London to Hear Free Music

There are many places in London that offer opportunities to hear free music. Here's our list of the best places to hear free music in London:

St Martin-in-the-Fields at lunch time every day Covent Garden Market on the lower levels Buskers (street performers) on the South Bank of the River Southbank Centre St James Church in Piccadilly – Free music recitals at 1:10pm on Mondays, Wednesdays and Fridays.

66. People Watching is Free!

If you're short on cash while in Britain and want something to do, people watching is free!

If you want to just sit around and watch London go by, grab a sandwich and sit on the steps to the National Gallery in Trafalgar Square for some of the best people watching in London, or check out Hyde Park.

If you're outside of London, pick any high street or central business area, and you're bound to be entertained. Most public squares are next to free attractions, so you can take advantage of those as well!

67. Budget Tip: Read Local British Newspapers to Discover Free and Fun Local Events

Wherever you are in Britain, there's still a vibrant local newspaper industry. Pick up a cheap local newspaper, and you're bound to find something free and fun to do while you're there. This is especially useful in London where newspapers like the Evening Standard will have a ton of free and fun things to do in their Friday editions.

So, when in Rome, do as the Romans do, and read the local paper. Personally, I like to read local papers just to get a feel for the area and what life is like there. Some of the quirkiest and most interesting events are local matters that don't get much press outside of Britain - or even their county! Reading the local paper is like peeling away a layer of the community and peeking inside. It's a great way to transition from being a tourist to a traveler.

68. Book a Dinner and Theatre Combo Deal

If you're looking for a good deal on a date night in London and want to do a nice dinner and take in a show, consider doing a dinner/theatre combo deal. Often you can get a nice dinner in a restaurant as well as theatre seats, so you get one great night out for one discounted price.

This is a great way to save money on both the dinner as well as the show itself.

Start browsing here:

http://www.londontown.com/TheatreAndDinner

69. Top 5 Free Things to do in Leicester, England

Leicester is a vibrant and fun city to visit, so we've put together our list of the top 5 sites that you shouldn't miss in Leicester, England.

Charnwood Museum - Situated in the pleasant Queen's Park, Charnwood Museum features permanent exhibitions that have been grouped into four areas: Coming to Charnwood, The Natural World of Charnwood, Living off the Land, and Earning a Living.

Gas Museum, National Gas Museum Trust - The largest museum in the world devoted to gas! Gas appliances and equipment.

Leicester Royal Infirmary: History Museum - Covers the fascinating history of medicine. **Belgrave Hall Museum & Gardens** - Stunning home that tells the history of Leicester.

Abbey Pumping Station - Abbey Pumping Station is Leicester's Museum of Science and Technology, displaying Leicester's industrial, technological and scientific heritage.

70. Top 5 Free Things to do in Aberdeen, Scotland

Aberdeen is not known for being hot on the tourist trail in Britain, but if you find yourself traveling that far north, there's plenty to see and do on a budget. Here's our list of the top free things to do in Aberdeen.

Aberdeen Art Gallery - Aberdeen's splendid Art Gallery houses an important fine art collection with particularly good examples of 19th-, 20th- and 21st-century works, a rich and diverse applied art collection, an exciting program of special exhibitions, a gallery shop and café.

Aberdeen Maritime Museum - Aberdeen Maritime Museum tells the story of the city's long relationship with the sea. This award-winning museum is located on the historic Shiprow and incorporates Provost Ross's House, which was built in 1593. The Maritime Museum houses a unique collection covering shipbuilding, fast sailing ships, fishing and port history.

Provost Skene's House - Dating from 1545, Provost Skene's House now houses an attractive series of period rooms, furnished to show how people lived in the 17th, 18th and early 19th centuries.

Aberdeenshire Farming Museum - Award-winning portrayal of regional farming history over the past 200 years and Hareshowe working farm.

Explore Aberdeen's Parks - Aberdeen has many beautiful parks and gardens that are free to enjoy.

Chapter 7

SHOPPING

Who doesn't love to shop? With careful planning, you can still have fun shopping in Britain on a budget. Our tips will help you make the most of every pound.

71. Pay Attention to your Coins

If you are traveling to Britain from the United States, one very common mistake that most Americans make, myself included, is not paying attention to the coins you receive as change while you are in Britain. Here in the United States, we usually only pay for items using paper money, so when you go to Britain you may find yourself doing the same thing. While it is perfectly acceptable to pay there using a paper note, keep in mind that some of the coins there have larger denominations than we do in the United States.

It is easy to throw your coins in your pocket and think of them as spare change, but they have £2 and £1 coins as well. At the end of the day, all of those coins can really add up. When you are handed coins, pay attention to what you are getting back. There can be some real value there.

If you are left with a lot of coins at the end of your trip, a great way to spend them is at the airport. Every time I go I end up with about £10-15 left from my visit, and I always spend it at the airport. Don't bother to exchange coins back into your normal currency; you'll loose horribly on the exchange rate normally. Go buy a local magazine or a sandwich. If you are still left over with some coins, they make wonderful souvenirs, too.

72. Buying Souvenirs on the Cheap

One of the most expensive aspects of traveling can be souvenir shopping. Just about everyone would love to take home a little something to remind them of their trip, and it seems that every tourist attraction has a shop to buy souvenirs. Many attractions even funnel traffic to exit through the gift shop to entice you. However, if you're a smart shopper, you will save money and have a wonderful souvenir to remember your trip.

My first suggestion is to avoid gift shops at attractions. Museums, history attractions, and other tourist venues always have gift shops. Most sell gifts that are unique to that specific attraction, and they also sell city souvenirs. For example, at the Tower of London they sell Tower souvenirs and London souvenirs. Don't buy your city-specific gifts here – they are way overpriced!

Set a budget BEFORE you go into the gift shop. I usually give myself a budget for the day making sure to include some spending money in case I see something I like. Keeping this in mind, I usually allow one large splurge, or expensive souvenir from the trip.

While I do not suggest buying city-specific items at gift shops in popular attractions, there are some gifts that can only be bought there. For example, an art print at a museum or a replica of the crown jewels at the Tower of London. If the souvenir is relevant to the attraction, chances are you aren't going to find it anywhere else, so buy it.

My last suggestion is to shop at the airport. Most large airports, especially when flying internationally, offer duty-free shopping. Avoiding the hefty VAT tax is a huge plus. I always do my souvenir shopping at the airport. Heathrow especially has awesome shopping. I can get all of my Harrods souvenirs at a fraction of the price, and I get all my London gear there, too.

Things to keep in mind: be choosey, shop for price, and don't be afraid to splurge at specific attractions. Also remember that you must travel home with whatever you buy. A fragile souvenir may be a great gift, but consider how you are going to get it home. Can you carry it on the airplane? Last but not least, remember that you want something special to remind you of the unique experiences that you've had.

73. Shopping Tip: Don't Buy British DVDs – They Won't Work at Home

DVDs are region-coded, and British DVDs are in a different video format than US TV sets. While most DVD players can convert the video format, you won't be able to play them in America unless you've purchased a "region-free" DVD player.

Most new Bluray DVDs are not region-coded, but this varies by manufacturer. It's better to not take the risk unless you own a region-free DVD player.

Some souvenir shops will sell region-free DVDs aimed at tourists. It's OK to buy these, but double-check the packaging. If not, save your money and buy the same DVD when you get home.

CDs are OK to buy.

74. Don't Convert to Dollars at Checkout

A new feature in a lot of stores these days is that when they swipe your American (or foreign) credit card, they'll offer to convert your purchase to dollars on the spot rather than process your purchase in British pounds.

You would think that this would be a better deal for you if you can get the lowest exchange rate – at least that's what these companies want you to think. You won't get a good exchange rate, and the premium you pay just lines the pockets of the store.

When a check out person asks you if you want to convert to dollars, politely decline and have the transaction run in British pounds. In the end, you'll get a better deal. Or if you want an even better deal, just pay cash.

75. Hold Onto Your Receipts for a VAT Refund at the Airport

It's no secret that Britain's 20% VAT (or sales tax) hurts when traveling in Britain. It inflates the costs of everything in Britain, and you don't notice it because it's built into every price - so things just seem more expensive all around.

You can, however, get some of the VAT back at the airport when you leave Britain. But you have to do a little legwork to get it.

You need to shop at a retailer that supports the VAT refund scheme, so ask. Most major retailers and department stores will be participating in the program. They'll have to give you a special form that you take with your receipt to the airport.

Once you get to the airport and get through security, find the customs window and give them all your paperwork. You should get a voucher for a refund at one of the currency exchanges. You may also have to actually have the items with you at the counter. It's a lot of hassle, but if you spent a lot of money shopping while in Britain, it's worth doing.

One special note: you can't claim VAT back on services like your hotel stay. We tried once. Doesn't work.

76. VAT-Free Shopping at Harrods in London - Save 20% off your Purchase!

To save time and hassle, the department store Harrods actually allows you to shop VAT free.

If you spend more than £50 in the store, you can claim back your VAT in the store itself rather than having to save your receipts and do it at the airport. If you plan to buy a lot of souvenirs or do any other shopping there, then this is a great deal.

If you spend £100 in Harrods, you get £20 back – not a bad deal! If you plan on making any large purchases, Harrods is the place to do it while in London. To take advantage of this, you'll need your passport with you when you shop.

77. Shop at Local Markets - Avoid Touristy Markets

You can save a lot of money on food and souvenirs if you shop at local markets in Britain, but watch out for markets geared at tourists – you won't save any money there.

Here are two examples of each:

Borough Market, London - A rich market, frequented by locals that offers foods, goods and more. It's at the top of the list for locals markets in London.

Jubilee Market Covent Garden, London - A market geared toward tourists right off Covent Garden. Locals don't frequent this, and everything is pretty overpriced. Same goes for the Portobello Road Market.

There are markets all throughout Britain. Some will be more touristy than others, but you can easily identify them. If there are locals about doing their shopping, there's good value for your money. If all you hear is American or foreign accents, you won't get good value for your money.

78. Candy Makes a Great Souvenir for Family Back Home

If you're traveling in Britain on a budget and are looking for the perfect gift for friends and family back home, consider getting them British candy.

British candy makes a great souvenir, because it's not very expensive, won't get seized by customs, and in general British candy is more tasty than American candy. Flavors are richer as is the chocolate. It has something to do with humidity.

It's easy to find. You can find it in any grocery or convenience store or even at the airport on your way back home. Pick up some Aero and Mars Bars, and consider your friends and family chuffed they'll be getting tasty British candy.

79. Looking for British Books On a Budget? Try Used Bookstores

I love browsing bookstores when I'm in Britain. There are so many interesting books published there that we don't get here in the USA, so I always feel like a kid in a candy store. It's easy to spend too much money on books (and overload my luggage!).

One way to keep things in check while book shopping in Britain is to stick to used book shops. There's a ton of them in London and Britain's other major cities, and you can usually get the same books in new condition for pennies on the pound.

I usually avoid the big chains like Waterstones or WH Smith and stick to used book shops. There's also a great used book market under Waterloo Bridge in London.

80. Avoid Buying Music CDs

While you won't have a problem using a CD bought in Britain back home, our question is why bother to buy music while in the UK at all? Sure, you can discover some music you haven't heard before, but who even buys CDs these days to discover music?

You can discover plenty of music using iTunes or any of the other digital music services, and buying music there is much cheaper than buying a CD (and then lugging it home). Just make note of the music you discover while in Britain, and then buy it digitally when you get back home.

81. Duty-Free Shopping at the Airport Isn't Always a Great Deal

While there are some things worth waiting to buy at the airport (i.e. cheap souvenirs), we don't really recommend doing a lot of duty-free shopping at the airports in Britain.

Duty-free shopping makes it seem like you're getting a deal as you don't have to pay sales (or VAT) or any other taxes on items you buy while in transit. It's been our experience, though, that prices are still higher than what you'd pay on the high street in Britain.

Even high dollar items like computers and cameras are way more expensive at the airport. I've never really been tempted by any good deals, because they're aren't any.

Besides, if you're leaving Britain, chances are you've spent all your vacation money enjoying your trip. Why save it for the airport, which is basically a mall that you can't leave once you enter?

82. Top 5 Free Things to do in Edinburgh, Scotland

If you're lucky enough to be able to venture north and visit the lovely land of Scotland, we've put together a list of the top free things to do in Edinburg. There's much to do!

Museum of Edinburgh - The Museum of Edinburgh is the city's treasure box – a maze of historic rooms crammed full of iconic objects from the capital's past.

The Scottish Parliament - See how government works in Scotland, explore this amazing new building, and take advantage of the free tours. Only open during certain times.

Scottish National Gallery and Portrait Gallery - Explore these world-class art museums with an awesome selection of western art.

St Giles' Cathedral - Standing halfway between Edinburgh Castle and the Palace of Holyroodhouse, St Giles' Cathedral was founded in the 12th century. Due to its role in Scotland's Reformation history, it is often referred to as the "Cradle of Presbyterianism."

The National Museum of Scotland - You can explore the entire world in this one museum - just reopened after a huge renovation.

83. Top 5 Free Things to do in Brighton, England

Brighton is Britain's seaside paradise. While it does have a reputation for having London prices, there's still plenty you can do for free to enjoy your time in this seaside resort. Here's our list of free things you can do in Brighton.

Beach - Brighton's famous beaches are free! **Brighton Pier** - One of the most spectacular piers in Britain is free to enter and enjoy.

Brighton Museum and Art Gallery - After a recent renovation, there's a great selection of art in this world-class gallery.

Booth Museum of Natural History - Explore the natural history of Britain and the south coast at

this great museum.

Do the undercliff walk - Stretching from Brighton Marina to Saltdean, the impressive undercliff walk is a popular and scenic coastal walk.

84. Top 5 Free Things To Do in Belfast, Northern Ireland

Northern Ireland doesn't have the reputation has a tourist hotspot, but now that their "troubles" have all but gone, there's much rich history to see in Northern Ireland. We thought it would be fun to put together a list of the top five free sites in Belfast.

Belfast Botanic Gardens - Occupying 28 acres of south Belfast, the gardens are popular with office workers, students and tourists.

Ulster Museum - The Ulster Museum, located in the Botanic Gardens in Belfast, has around 8,000 square metres of public display space, featuring material from the collections of fine art and applied art, archaeology, ethnography, treasures from the Spanish Armada, local history, numismatics, industrial archaeology, botany, zoology and geology.

Northern Ireland in the Second World War Memorial Building – Unique memorial dedicated to Northern Ireland's participation in World War II.

Armagh County Museum - The displays focus on the history, natural history and culture of County Armagh and include archaeological artifacts; historic domestic tools and items; textiles and costumes including military uniforms, ceramics, natural history and geology specimens; and railway memorabilia.

Giant's Causeway – A unique geological formation that's steeped in myth and legend.

Chapter 8

COMMUNICATION

Keeping in touch with home while you're in Britain is a great way to maintain a comfortable trip. The problem is that it's very expensive to do so. Here are some tips that will offset those costs.

85. How to Call Britain or London Cheaply - Use Skype

If you're planning a trip to Britain and need to call somewhere in the UK to make arrangements, you'll most likely get sticker shock when you get the phone bill. Thankfully, with the advent of modern technology, this doesn't need to happen.

We use the free service Skype to make all of our calls to the UK. If the person you're calling uses Skype, it's completely free. However, you can also call regular phones using Skype, and then you pay a small per-minute fee. The fee is currently 2.3 cents per minute from the USA, which is a great deal to call the UK.

This is especially useful for transatlantic couples or anyone else that will spend a lot of time on the phone with the UK.

86. Budget Tips: How to Call Home from London For Free

When we travel, we always try to stay in touch with home. The problem is that this can be very expensive if you're not careful. Avoid using your mobile phone, making calls from the hotel, or using pay phones, as these are the most expensive options.

You can call home for free using Skype, too. Setup an account before you go, and have your friends and family do the same. It costs nothing to make Skype-to-Skype calls. You can even call from a mobile phone that supports it (like an iPhone), so it's just like talking on a phone. Or you can call for free from your computer (assuming you have access to WiFi).

If your friends and family don't have Skype, you can call them like you would on a phone and you'll only pay a few cents a minute.

You can also use Skype to make really cheap local calls while in Britain, which is really useful for booking tickets or arranging travel. You can actually use the service to get a local UK number (costs $18 for 3 months).

We won't travel any other way now. Website: http://skype.com

87. Budget Tip: Whatever you Do, Don't Use Your iPhone in Britain

If you travel to Britain with your iPhone, you may be very excited to be using it on a foreign trip. You have probably even loaded it with useful apps for your trip. Our warning is to be careful how you use it.

International roaming data charges will put you in the poorhouse. We used our iPhone on one first trip and returned home to a $1200 phone bill.

If you really want to use your iPhone while in Britain, here's a few tips to follow:

Only buy apps that store their data locally. Turn off international roaming before you leave. Take advantage of free wifi. Buy an international roaming package from AT&T. Turn off email or anything else that uses Push notifications. Avoid using Google Maps. GPS is free, but the data for loading the maps is not. Avoid text messages as they costs a lot more than texts at home

Your best bet may be to rent a local UK phone or buy a prepaid phone. You could also just leave it at home and enjoy your vacation without it – plenty of people traveled to Britain without iPhones before they existed!

88. Cheap Cell Phone Rental While in the UK - Tep Wireless

Since we do a lot of business in the UK while we're there, it makes sense for us to rent a mobile phone while we're in town. We get a local phone number, a smartphone, and it makes it a lot easier for people to get a hold of us.

I tried to rely on Skype a few trips ago when I was in London. It worked if I was in the room, but when I was out and about I had trouble keeping in touch with various business associates.

Now I rent a mobile phone from Tep Wireless, which offers UK smartphones for rent as well as Mobile WiFi units. You get a local phone number and a way to access your email from anywhere while in London. The WiFi hotspot also works great with the iPhone and is worth the extra cost.

Pricing starts at $5.95 a day for the smartphone or $5.95 a day for a mobile WiFi. Check out their website: http://www.tepwireless.com/

89. Don't Waste Your Money on a Travel Voltage Converter

We fell for this when we first started traveling to Britain. We bought an expensive power/voltage converter for electrical devices. While there many be instances where this is useful, we have never used it and threw it away long ago to free up the luggage space.

Britain does use three-pronged plugs that are different from plugs in the USA or the rest of the world. We recommend picking up a couple of cheap adapters at Wal-mart or Target. They will be all you need.

Most electronic devices can convert the power already. Most computers and laptops do this, and smaller devices all have standard chargers these days anyway. So learn from our mistake, and don't buy the voltage converter – you just won't need it.

90. Don't Waste Money on an Airplane Charger for Your Laptop or iPad

Years ago, I bought a special charger for my laptop for use on an airplane. It was not cheap. I've never used it. Learn from this mistake.

Most laptops these days have a long battery life. You can get a good amount of use out of them on the plane, so there's usually no need to charge your device in the air.

Many planes now have standard American pronged plugs in the seats, so you don't need special adapters anymore. This can vary by airline and class you're traveling in.

We recommend charging your devices fully before you leave and taking advantage of free plugs in the airport itself. If you really absolutely need to stay charged, you can buy an extra battery or a power pack, and you shouldn't have a problem.

If you're using a device like an iPhone or iPad (which already have long battery life), most airlines are incorporating USB charging ports in their seats as well.

91. Top 5 Free Things to do in Coventry, England

Coventry is at the heart of England and features much rich history and attractions worth a visit. Though much of the city was destroyed during World War II, there's still plenty of heritage in the city centre.

Take a walk along medieval Spon Street - Step back in time with a walk down medieval Spon Street. Shops and bars include a local butcher, an art gallery and the Old Windmill pub.

Coventry Transport Museum - From the penny farthing to the DeLorean sports car, the Transport Museum hosts a history of road transport.

Relax in Coventry's peaceful Memorial Park - The park hosts various events, including the annual Godiva Festival in June.

Visit the Herbert Museum and Art Gallery - The Herbert has undergone a £20 million redevelopment. It's now a major local attraction which highlights Coventry as a major city for arts and heritage.

Coventry Cathedral - The gothic cathedral was destroyed during WWII, but the ruins are still there – right next to the gleaming new cathedral that rose from the ashes. Very moving visit!

92. Top 5 Free Things to do in Bournemouth, England

We love Dorset, and one of our favorite cities is Bournemouth. If you're on a budget, there's plenty to see and do for free if you poke around. We've put together a list of the top five things you can do for free in Bournemouth.

Pier to Pier walk - Start at either Bournemouth or Boscombe Pier and finish at the other. Enjoy the scenic stroll along the promenade and treat yourself to coffee and cake at one of the many cafes, restaurants, or hotels at either end.

Russell-Cotes Art Gallery & Museum - Visit one of the most important and fascinating museum- houses in England. It holds collections of international status and reflects the Victorian fascination with world cultures.

Swim in the Sea - It's free to swim in the Atlantic Ocean and enjoy Bournemouth's beaches.

Bournemouth's Parks & Gardens - Bournemouth's Gardens are split into three areas of Victorian beauty: starting with the Lower Gardens adjacent to the sea and leading to the Central Gardens in the town centre, and then the Upper Gardens.

Poole Museum (next to Bournemouth) - Formerly known as the Waterfront Museum, this local history museum situated on the Lower High Street in the Old Town area of Poole, Dorset is part of the Borough of Poole Museum Service.

Chapter 9

OTHER TRAVEL TIPS

Our final roundup of Budget Tips to help you make the most of your trip to Britain!

93. Use ATMs to Get Local Currency and Avoid Currency Exchanges

The cheapest way to get money exchanged in Britain is to just use your ATM card to take money directly out of the ATM (the Brits call them cashpoints).

Currency exchanges are usually a rip-off and have the worst exchange rates, so we don't recommend taking a lot of US Dollars with you to Britain and exchanging them there. Banks get the best inter-market exchange rates and pass that on through the ATM network.

Also, most ATMs in London are free, so you'll probably only be charged a withdrawal fee by your bank.

Leave your dollars at home.

94. Traveling With Credit Cards in Britain - Watch out for Hidden Fees

We've written before about relying on ATM cards to get cash while in Britain – you'll get the best exchange rate this way. What what about using your credit cards, too?

This is a little more complicated.

On the one hand, you'll get the best exchange rate when you swipe your credit card as you would when you use an ATM. However, credit cards tack on foreign conversion fees that effectively hide what's basically a higher exchange rate. They've gotten in trouble for this recently and have cut back the fees.

Before choosing which credit cards to take with you to Britain (and you should take more than one), check your credit card terms and conditions for information on what fees you'll pay when you swipe abroad. You may even have to call them.

Also, some cashiers in the UK may look at your card a little strangely when you pay. A Chip & Pin system is now standard in the UK, so most credit cards don't get swiped. Instead, you set your card in a reader and enter a PIN number. The problem for Americans is that our cards don't work with this system, so you have to tell the cashier to swipe instead.

95. Don't Carry all of your Money with You

Don't carry all of your money on you when out and about. It's a good idea to hide some money in

your luggage or in your room. But hide small amounts only! Large amounts should be in the hotel safe. You just want to make sure not to have all of your money in one place!

I would also not carry all your credit cards on you either. You'll be less tempted to spend, and you'll be much safer if something bad happens.

96. Stock up on Camera Memory Cards and Batteries before Leaving

One mistake we made a few years ago was thinking that if we ran out of memory card space on our digital cameras, we could just buy some while in Britain. This was an expensive mistake.

We recommend stocking up on memory cards at home before you depart for Britain. They're cheap these days, so buy more than you think you need so you're not afraid to take as many pictures as your heart desires. We travel with a half a dozen 4gb memory cards, and we haven't run out of space yet.

Also, depending on the make and model of your camera, be sure to stock up on plenty of batteries or a spare rechargeable battery. One of our previous cameras used rechargeable batteries. We only had one with us in Britain, and we ran out of a charge in the middle of sightseeing. A replacement in Britain was eyewateringly expensive.

97. Budget Tips: How to Find Free Public Toilets in Britain

Many Americans are shocked to find that when they travel to Britain for the first time, a lot of public toilets charge for the privilege of their use. That's not something very commonplace in the USA.

The Brits have their reasons for charging: it keeps the bathrooms cleaner and keeps out undesirables (like drug addicts shooting up). But it can be annoying if you're caught short, and you don't have the exact change to pay for access to a loo.

Luckily, there's a resource you can use called Find a Public Toilet. Not all the toilets listed are free, but it will show you the free ones in any given town in Britain. It's a great resource. Most major towns will have free public toilets. Many businesses will have them, too, and they'll be clearly marked.

Check out Find a Public Toilet:
http://www.findatoilet.mobi/

98. How About Avoiding London All Together?

This tip will be controversial, but if you're really looking to travel around Britain on a budget, avoid going to London all together.

London is one of the world's most expensive cities. Much travel in Britain revolves around it, but if you've been there before and want to see more of Britain, you can skip it.

Most major international airlines fly direct into Birmingham, Cardiff, Manchester or Edinburgh airports. Rather than land in London, you land in the heart of Britain with many options to explore the countryside off the beaten path. Best of all: you don't have to deal with the madness at Heathrow or deal with the expense of just getting out of Heathrow.

99. Top 5 Free Things to do in Plymouth, England

Plymouth is full of rich Maritime history and is best known as the departure point for the Pilgrims who settled Massachusetts. So what better way to enjoy Plymouth than to gather together the Top 5 free things to do if you're in town?

Plymouth City Museum and Art Gallery - The museums permanent galleries display extensive collections of fine art, human history and natural history.

St Andrews Church - There has been a church on this site for almost 1200 years. During heavy bombing in World War II, the church was left a burnt out shell but was reconstructed in 1957.

HM Naval base Devonport - Tour the base and see where today's modern warships are repaired and serviced. Step aboard a warship or nuclear submarine and experience how sailors live and work aboard.

The Barbican & Sutton Harbour (Mayflower port) - Plymouth's old port area, now a bustling community of specialist shops, craft workshops and art galleries. The Pilgrim Fathers departure for the New World is commemorated here at the Mayflower Steps.

Waterfront Walkway - A walk along the Plymouth's Waterfront Walkway allows you to explore the history and magnificent setting of the maritime city.

100. Top 5 Free Things to do in Dover, England

Dover has been the gateway to Britain for thousands of years, and as a result has a rich and iconic history. The White Cliffs of Dover are a symbol of Britain and are worth visiting Dover alone. Here's our list of the top five free things to do in Dover, England.

Samphire Hoe - Interesting walks and cycle rides in an amazing place – the best place to view the White Cliffs!

White Cliffs - Spectacular views and miles of stunning cliff top walks.

De Bradelei Wharf - Superb shopping in a maritime setting.

Battle of Britain Memorial - Visit the national memorial to the aircrew who won the Battle of Britain.

Western Heights - Walk around extensive 18th- and 19th-century fortifications.

101. Don't Forget to Have Fun!

We've written quite a few words on doing Britain on a budget, but I think for our final budget tip, we'll stick to this:

Don't forget to have fun! Having fun doesn't cost a dime!

Don't spend your whole trip counting every penny to the point where you've sucked all joy out of the experience.

Believe me, we've been there. We been on trips to Britain where we literally ran out of money, but you know what? We still managed to have a good time. And we still keep going back.

The goal of our budget tips guide was to show that with careful planning and having a wide breadth of knowledge of travel issues you'll face, you can save some serious money while traveling in Britain and still having a great time.

Have fun! Or else what's the point of even going?

Appendix 1

101 Free Things to do in Britain

1. **British Museum** - The best Museum in London. Plan a whole day here.
2. **National Museum Cardiff** - Dedciated to Welsh History and Culture
3. **St Fagans: National History Museum** – An open-air museum in Cardiff chronicling the historical lifestyle, culture and architecture of the Welsh people
4. **National Gallery** – Some of history's best art for free.
5. **Trafalgar Square** – Go see Nelson and people-watch as London goes by.
6. **Walk through Hyde Park** - No trip to London is complete without a walk through Hyde Park.
7. **Covent Garden** – Explore the old market, watch street performers, hear musicians. Plenty of free fun to be had in Covent Garden!
8. **Tate Modern** – Some of the art is questionable, but the building is amazing in itself and worth a visit alone.
9. **Museum of Science & Industry Manchester** – A large museum devoted to the development of science, technology, and

industry with emphasis on the city's achievements in these fields

10. **Evensong Church Service** – You have to pay admission to get into most of London's cathedrals, but if you go to evensong service you can get in for free.

11. **Ulster Museum** - Located in Belfast – it features many wonderful exhibitions on Northern Irish history.

12. **Cross Tower Bridge** - It's a free thrill for all tourists to cross the bridge! Wait around, and you might even see it open and close.

13. **National Maritime Museum** – Explore Britain Royal Navy's history.

14. **Walk through the Woolwich Foot Tunnel** – Cross one of the oldest tunnels under the Thames – get off a the DLR stop King George V and walk to the entrance.

15. **Pollocks Toy Museum** – Toys from around the world – great place for the kids!

16. **Imperial War Museum** – See Britain's Military History in all its glory.

17. **Imperial War Museum North** – Located in Manchester this is one of the five branches of the Imperial War Museum, the museum explores the impact of modern conflicts on people and society.

18. **Borough Market** – Explore one of London's coolest markets!

19. **National Railway Museum** – In York – dedicated to Britain rich Rail History

20. **The National Railway Museum at Shildon** – A Branch of the National Railway Museum in Durham

21. **Museum of London** – Fun look at the history of London.

22. **National Portrait Gallery** – Might not interest everyone as it's pictures of aristocracy through the ages.

23. **Natural History Museum** – One of the world's finest natural history museums. Check out the Darwin Centre!

24. **Victoria and Albert Museum** – A strange hodge-podge museum that provides an interesting insight into Britain's cultural heritage.

25. **Science Museum** – Who doesn't like science? Kids will love it!

26. **Tate Britain** - Like the National Gallery, it's home to some beautiful art.

27. **Guildhall Art Gallery** – Collection of art collected by the Corporation of London.

28. **Bank of England Museum** – Take a look at the monetary history of the world.

29. **Changing of the Guard** – It's a tourist trap, but always fun to see on a sunny day. Every day in the summer at 11:30. Arrive early.

30. **Kenwood House** – Lovely stately home located in Hampstead Heath.

31. **Geffrye Museum** – Period rooms museum from 1600 to today.

32. **Royal Air Force Museum** – See the history of Britain's flying aces.

33. **St James' Park** – One of London's fine Royal Parks.

34. **Scottish National Gallery** – Like the National Gallery in London except it's in Scotland (art is not necessarily related to Scotland)

35. **National Media Museum** – Located in West Yorkshire – it's dedicated to Britain's media heritage.

36. **Museum of Liverpool** – A new museum in Liverpool dedicated to it's history and impact on the world.

37. **Princess Diana Memorial** - Located in Hyde Park, you can pay your respects to Princess Di.

38. **National Museum of Scotland** – A museum in Edinburgh dedicated to Scotland's rich history and culture

39. **Speaker's Corner** - Arrive on a Sunday morning, and watch the colorful characters gathered to speak about anything.

40. **Leicester Square** – Relax in the park in the middle or admire the glitzy lights of this tourist haven.

41. National Football Museum -

42. **Museum of London Docklands** - A lesser known London, but cool none the less. You can explore London's maritime shipping history.

43. **Lunch Concerts at St. Martin in the Fields** – Enjoy lunch in the Crypt at St. Martin in the Fields, and also enjoy free concerts every day.

44. **Watch a TV Show Recorded at the BBC** – It's free to be in the studio audience of a show as it's being recorded.

45. **View London from Primrose Hill** – Admire the view from London's Primrose Hill.

46. **Hunterian Museum** – See a unique collection of animal specimens kept in jars.

47. **Foundling Museum** - Britain's original home for abandoned children and London's first ever public art gallery.

48. **Peter Pan Statue** – Check out the statue of the literary classic located in Kensington Gardens.

49. **Museum of Childhood** – Dedicated to the history of childhood.

50. **Touch the Roman Wall** – Throughout the city of London you'll see traces of the original Roman Wall fortification. There's large pieces around the Museum of London.

51. **Walk Across Hampstead Heath** – Beautiful park in London that provides lovely views of metropolitan London.

52. **Visit Regent's Park** – Another great Royal Park, and there's a zoo!

53. **Visit Platform 9 3/4** – Doesn't really exist, of course, but station authorities have set up a fake entrance for Harry Potter fans at King's Cross Station.

54. **Visit St Pancras International** – Admire this beautiful station, watch Eurostar trains arrive and depart, and visit the statue of the couple kissing.

55. **Walk along the South Bank** – Walk from Waterloo Bridge to the Tate Modern, and see a huge part of London.

56. **Walk through Richmond Park** – Another lovely park.

57. **Changing of the Guard in Windsor** - If you happen to be in Windsor, there's a changing of the guard there as well.

58. **Abbey Road Crosswalk** - Become a traffic hazard, and have your own Beatles pictures taken.

59. **Postman's Park** - The square from the movie "Closer" where memorials are dedicated to people who died saving Londoners.

60. **Explore Blue Plaques** - Look closely on old buildings, and you'll see lots of blue plaques, which offer some history about famous people who lived there.

61. **Visit the Cenotaph** – Pay respects to Britain's memorials to the two World Wars.

62. **Picnic in Battersea Park** – Lovely riverside park with views of the Thames.

63. **Cross the Jubilee Bridge** – Cross the Thames at Embankment on this beautiful bridge.

64. **Cross the Millennium Bridge** – Best way to cross from the Tate Modern to St Paul's or vice verse.

65. **See the Roosevelt & Churchill Statue** - Located in Bond Street, see the two great world leaders as friends.

66. **See the Churchill Statue** – Located in Parliament Square.

67. **See the Lincoln Statue** - Statue of the American president located in Parliament Square. The only one to have such an honor.

68. **Free WiFi in the Apple Stores** – Need wifi or access to the web? Then stop in the Apple Stores in Covent Garden or Regent Street and recharge your Internet batteries.

69. **Get Photographed in a Red Phone Box** – Nothing more touristy or more awesome than a picture in a red phone box.

70. **Visit the National Army Museum** – Discover the history of Britain's armed forces.

71. **Visit Russell Square** – Quiet little green park in the middle of bustling London right around the corner from the British Museum.

72. **Arbeia Roman Fort and Museum** – Excavated Roman remains, stunning reconstructions of original buildings and finds discovered at the Fort combine to give a unique insight into life in Roman Britain.

73. **Birmingham Museum and Art Gallery** – There are over 40 galleries to explore that display art, applied art, social history, archaeology and ethnography. The art gallery is famous for its Pre-Raphaelite paintings, which are part of the largest public Pre-Raphaelite collection in the world.

74. **Cerne Abbas Giant** – A huge outline sculpted into the chalk hillside above the village of Cerne Abbas representing a naked, sexually aroused, club-wielding giant. Public

perceptions are wide-ranging, is he smutty, humorous or offensive?

75. **The Giant's Causeway, County Antrim, Northern Ireland** – Steeped in Legend which has it that Giant's used it to cross to Ireland.

76. **Great North Museum: Hancock** – Highlights of this award winning museum include a large-scale, interactive model of Hadrian's Wall, major displays showing the wonder and diversity of the animal and plant kingdoms, spectacular objects from the Ancient Greeks and mummies from Ancient Egypt, a planetarium and a life-size T-Rex dinosaur skeleton and much more.

77. **Hadrian's Wall** – The ancient Roman Wall that runs across Northern England

78. **Houghton House, Bedfordshire** – Romantic Ruin of a great stately home.

79. **International Slavery Museum** - Liverpool – A pretty grisley topic for a musuem but sure to be interesting.

80. **Laycock Village** – A Wiltshire village that's famous for being featured in Pride and Prejudice, Harry Potter, Cranford and much more!

81. **Letocetum Roman Baths and Museum** – Explore the remains of this once important

Roman staging post, including 'mansio' (Roman inn) and bathhouse.

82. **The National Slate Museum** – Museum in Wales dedicated to the Welsh slate industry.

83. **The National Wool Museum** – A museum in Wales dedicated to the Wool industry

84. **The Old House, Hereford** – The Old House is a remarkably well preserved example of a 17th Century timber-framed building and is situated in the heart of Hereford, surrounded by the commercial centre of the city. It is a startling sight, standing as the sole reminder of times-gone-by in the middle of a modern shopping precinct.

85. **Whipsnade Tree Cathedral** – This incredible tree cathedral was created after the First World War in a spirit of 'faith, hope and reconciliation'.

86. **Woolwich Ferry** – The Woolwich ferry is a free service operating between Woolwich and North Woolwich, linking the north and south circular roads across the Thames.

87. **Yorkshire Sculpture Park** – This is an outdoor catalog of 20th and 21st century British sculpture that covers over 500 acres of rolling countryside on the edge of the Yorkshire Dales.

88. **State Opening of Parliament** – See traditions that go back thousands of years and glimpse the Queen as she opens the new session of Parliament.

89. **Free Concerts at Wales Millenium Centre** – Check their schedule for frequent free concerts.

90. **See the Angel of the North** – Check out Anthony Gormley's iconic statue near Newcastle.

91. **Walk the Southwest Coast Path** – You don't need to walk the whole path to experience Britain's breathtaking coastline.

92. **Visit Chesil Beach** – Check out this iconic and strange geological formation in Dorset.

93. **Jurassic Coas**t – Glimpse fossils and rock formations in the rocks of Dorset's Coast.

94. **Visit Gold Hill** – Check out the iconic 'Hovis' Gold Hill as seen in the bread adverts.

95. **Tate St. Ives** – The St. Ives Branch of the Tate Art Museum Group.

96. **Visit Sherwood Forset** – Explore the haunt of Robin Hood and see the famous tree that bears his name.

97. **The Bristol & Bath Railway Path** – The Bristol & Bath Railway Path is a 21 km long traffic-free route along a disused railway path

between Bristol and Bath, perfect for a family day out.

98. **Iron Bridge Gorge** – See the iconic Bridge that ignited the industrial revolution. Access to the bridge is free but there are paid attractions there.

99. **Maiden Castle, Dorset** – This colossal Iron Age hill fort – the largest in Britain – is one of the many unmanned and free sites managed by English Heritage.

100. **The Winter Garden, Sheffield** – A vast temperate glasshouse in the centre of Sheffield, containing more than 2,500 plants from around the world.

101. **Royal Armouries Museum in Leeds** – Royal Armouries is the United Kingdom's National Museum of Arms and Armour, including artillery.

Appendix 2:

Useful LinksOur Websites:

Anglotopia: http://anglotopia.net

Londontopia: http://londontopia.net

Budget Britain Guide:
http://budgetbritainguide.com

Top 100 UK Attractions:
http://top100ukattractions.com

Top 100 UK Hotels: http://top100ukhotels.com

Travel Websites:

British Airways: http://ba.com/

Virgin Atlantic: http://virginatlantic.com/

Kayak.com: http://kayak.com/

Cheapoair.com: http://cheapoair.com/

Golden Tours: http://goldentours.com

Hostelbookers: http://hostelbookers.com/

Tep Wireless: http://tepwireless.com/

London Pass: http://londonpass.com

ABOUT ANGLOTOPIA

Anglotopia.net is the world's largest gathering place for Anglophiles. Founded in 2007 by Jonathan and Jacqueline Thomas as a hobby it grew to become a massive online community of dedicated Anglophiles. Jonathan and Jacqueline now work full time on Anglotopia and its sister websites. They travel to the UK at least once a year to do research.

Made in the USA
Charleston, SC
18 August 2012